THIRTEENWEEKGUITAR
TECHNIQUEBOOTCAMP

ADVANCED LEVEL

Your 13 Week Practice Plan to Master Picking, Legato, Sweeping & Tapping

CHRISBROOKS

FUNDAMENTALCHANGES

Thirteen Week Guitar Technique Bootcamp – Advanced Level

Your 13 Week Practice Plan to Master Picking, Legato, Sweeping & Tapping

ISBN: 978-1-78933-431-9

Published by **www.fundamental-changes.com**

Copyright © 2024 Christopher A. Brooks

Edited by Tim Pettingale

www.fundamental-changes.com

Join our free Facebook Community of Cool Musicians

www.facebook.com/groups/fundamentalguitar

Tag us for a share on Instagram: **FundamentalChanges**

Facebook: **ChrisBrooksGuitar**

Instagram: **FundamentalChanges**

Instagram: **chrisbrooksguitarist**

For over 350 Free Guitar Lessons with Videos Check Out

www.fundamental-changes.com

Cover Image Copyright: Shutterstock

Contents

Introduction 4

Get the Audio and Video 6

Week One: Refresher Course 7

Week Two: Alternate Picking 19

Week Three: Legato 28

Week Four: Economy Picking 36

Week Five: Scale Routine 43

Week Six: Sweep Picking Arpeggios.. 52

Week Seven: Maintenance Program 63

Week Eight: Hybrid Picking... 70

Week Nine: Tapping 76

Week Ten: String Skipping Arpeggios 84

Week Eleven: Technique Combos... 92

Weeks Twelve and Thirteen: Final Etude... 98

Conclusion 102

About the Author.. 103

Introduction

If you've been following my series of practice books, comprised firstly of *Guitar Practice Warmup Routines* and followed up by the *Thirteen Week Guitar Technique Bootcamp (Intermediate Level)*, welcome back!

If this is your first purchase in the series, here's what you missed…

With ninety-two exercises divided into ten routines, *Guitar Practice Warmup Routines* focuses on beginning your daily practice in the best way possible, using warmup time to loosen up and develop good form and technique.

Each warmup routine has a purpose: prime your picking, improve chordal facility, coordinate the hands, stretch out the fingers, build fingerpicking and hybrid picking, refresh scale knowledge, etc.

The intermediate version of the *Thirteen Week Guitar Technique Bootcamp* handled technique in two main stages. Firstly, it laid the groundwork for a solid command of techniques like alternate, sweep and economy picking, legato, and tapping, with prescribed homework and practice plans for developing and advancing players.

Secondly, it revisited each of the previous techniques with new routines of material that edge closer to an advanced level, and delivered an overview of my speed practice system.

This brings us to the book before you now. In this new bootcamp, the focus is on hitting the woodshed and getting the work done promptly. Including a warmup, many routines can be completed in as little as thirty minutes, leaving time for revision or other areas of playing.

After a recap of Week One, the new routines in this book outline the same kind of material I use in my own practice. With a thirteen-week intensive program format, you'll edge closer to playing with freedom and confidence in each technique.

While I've designed a serious program for people who want serious results, you won't be hunched over your guitar for hours at a time. Pro players will keep their technique in top condition using material that cuts to the chase. Not many guitar legends have eight hours to practice like they did in their teens! Even if you only get time for a few licks per day, you'll still get further ahead than you are now.

Each routine has up to ten examples of real things I practice, but you'll eventually be able to strip many topics back to a handful of drills. When you know your challenges and how to address them, your process and your chops will improve.

Calling this book the "advanced" bootcamp might suggest a dividing wall between this material and the intermediate volume. The truth is, there's more overlap and gradient to guitar technique than fixed-level terminology might indicate.

While the motto of this book is most certainly "do the thing", I encourage you to jump back into the intermediate bootcamp any time you feel that a concept needs more time in the oven. It's essential to be honest and step back to move forward with more confidence and sure footing.

If you can commit to these new practice plans and put in some time almost every day, I'm confident that you'll be a more adept technician of the guitar in thirteen weeks.

Chris Brooks

How To Use This Book

Each chapter targets an element of technique for one week, using a series of related drills that form a practice routine. At the end of the chapter, I'll instruct you on how to approach the drills effectively over five to six days. You can take at least one day off to do something else!

Instead of drilling one lick to infinity, learning another, then another, like you might have in other books, you'll work through every exercise in these plans daily. This is far more effective than perfecting one lick before moving ahead – a far slower way to do things.

You mightn't be accustomed to working on several new licks on the go, but remember that we're practicing *skills*, not licks. The larger goal is to improve the technique at hand which, in turn, will improve your ability to master new licks, with success breeding success.

This practice format is what I call *Targeted Practice*. Much like "arm day" or "leg day" at the gym, targeted practice sessions focus on a specific skill for an entire session.

A sample week might look like this:

- Sunday – read the chapter through without playing

- Monday – run through each drill in the chapter in free time, paying attention to the notes and mechanical execution

- Tuesday to Friday – warm up, then run the suggested routine with the prescribed number of repeats and speeds for thirty minutes. Use any available time afterward to revise a previous topic

- Saturday – take a day off or study a subject of your choice

A common time-killer is doing too much "metronoming" using small increments which are often redundant. For example, if you can comfortably play an exercise at 120 bpm with good form and timing, spending fifteen minutes crawling from 80 bpm to 120 bpm kills a lot of valuable practice time.

The approach in this program will be more straightforward – three speeds per lick on repetition days, with enough variance in tempo to make a difference to your progress.

Week One is a refresher course in concepts from the intermediate book, so the first week's practice will be intensive revision. From there, you'll have one main technique focus per week.

In Chapter Seven, I'll show you how to construct a maintenance practice session to address several techniques in a single sitting.

To summarise, each chapter will look something like this:

- Material for the week

- Specifics of the technique for your attention

- Practice Plan

Don't forget to grab the audio (details on the next page) and log in to access the bonus video content. Besides selections from each chapter played on camera, you'll find bonus lessons mentioned as we go.

See you in the Week One chapter when you're all set up.

Get the Audio and Video

The audio files for this book are available to download for free from **www.fundamental-changes.com.** The link is in the top right-hand corner. Simply select this book title from the drop-down menu and follow the instructions to get the audio.

We recommend that you download the files directly to your computer, not to your tablet, and extract them there before adding them to your media library. On the download page, there is a help PDF, and we also provide technical support via the contact form.

There's a wealth of video material available to help you get the most out of this book, available at:

https://geni.us/bootcampadv

Sign up for free to access many examples from the book.

For over 350 free guitar lessons with videos check out:

www.fundamental-changes.com

Join our free Facebook Community of Cool Musicians

www.facebook.com/groups/fundamentalguitar

Tag us for a share on Instagram: **FundamentalChanges**

Week One: Refresher Course

This chapter summarizes essential points from the *Thirteen Week Guitar Technique Bootcamp (Intermediate)*. All examples offered are in the key of C Major unless otherwise stated.

Before the recap, a note about my fingering choices.

Diatonic scale shapes commonly have spacings of three types, made up of whole tones and semitones.

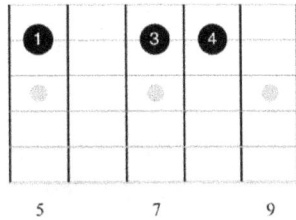

While the first two options below are almost always fretted with fingers one, two and four, the third layout has options (i.e. fingers one, three and four, or one, two and three). Which fingering you choose will depend on what's happening on the other strings or where you are along the fretboard.

Many drills include my fingering suggestions but feel free to make your own choices.

Two whole tones   Semitone + whole tone   Whole tone + semitone   or

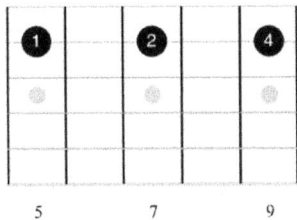

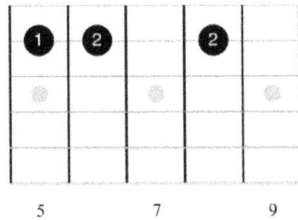

5   7   9   5   7   9   5   7   9   5   7   9

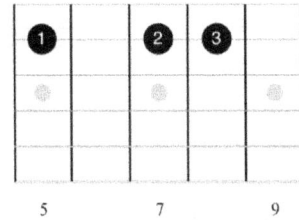

Since I won't be teaching all the techniques again from scratch in this book, use the examples below to determine if you're ready to forge ahead with the new routines or need to spend a little more time completing the last book.

For alternate picking, there are three main concepts to have a handle on:

1. Changing strings consistently after upstrokes

2. Changing strings consistently after downstrokes

3. Changing strings with a mixture of pick strokes

Each approach will benefit from a logical down/up motion along the strings with an effective transition to each new string.

Let's explore some chromatic picking runs that fit into each category above.

In Example 1a, since the pick leaves each string on an upstroke and arrives at the following string on a downstroke, it makes sense to pick along the axis you'll see in the video, where downstrokes go beneath the plane of the strings and upstrokes rise above them.

This way, going to higher or lower strings is possible with the same picking trajectory.

Example 1a:

On the flip side, Example 1b relies on getting downstrokes clear of the strings to access subsequent strings on upstrokes directly.

Example 1b:

When it comes to changing strings after a mix of upstrokes *and* downstrokes, the picking hand needs to be adept at working in between the strings (inside picking) and around them (outside picking).

As you watch the video for Example 1a, take note of the way I prepare the first pick stroke of each new string with the strokes leading up to it. The side-on video footage was recorded in slow-motion mode to capture the details often missed at moderate and high speeds.

Example 1c:

Moving to sweep picking, the previous bootcamp book included practice material on:

- Triad shapes with directional picking and rest strokes

- Changing direction using doubled notes

- Changing direction between strings using single notes

- Expanding major and minor triads to six-string shapes

Example 1d features a G Major triad in three-string and five-string portions.

With a small pause between direction changes in bars one and two, there's time to change your picking angle and switch from ascending to descending.

In the larger form, it becomes more challenging to change directions seamlessly at either end of the shape.

Playing these 1/8th note triplets above 160 bpm and into the ballpark of 200 bpm should give you a good sense of how well your direction changes are working.

Example 1d:

Example 1e reflects the more advanced material we looked at in Week Eleven of the intermediate bootcamp.

Here, the six-string A Minor and C Major triad shapes change direction at various points using single notes as the "turnaround" points.

Hammer-ons and pull-offs are used on the fifth string to keep the flow of the general sweep picking direction.

Example 1e:

Sweep-picked triads and alternate-picked scale lines can be combined as a test of your ability to switch techniques on command.

Example 1f:

Sweep picking makes a good segue into economy picking, a technique we developed in Week Six of the last bootcamp and expanded in Week Twelve.

Calling on the strengths of alternate and sweep picking, economy picking helped us establish the following precepts:

- The pick takes the most direct line of motion between strings

- Ascending strings begin with downstrokes and descending strings with upstrokes

- Sweep Picking is used to change strings any time the last pick stroke along a string can move through to the next string

To test your economy picking, compare this C Major scale run which is picked two ways: alternate picking in bars one and two; economy picking in bars three and four.

Aim for a good command of timing, accurate articulation, and some speed. It doesn't matter so much what your top speed is right now, but how closely you can match one approach to the other.

Example 1g:

Now try a longer major scale run that changes position and uses sweep picking for every string change.

Example 1h:

Since sweep and economy picking are more or less separate terms for the same directional approach, it's important to be competent at scale and triad combos like Example 1i.

Example 1i:

In fretting techniques, completing the legato checklist includes having good command of:

- Hammer-ons, pull-offs, and hammer-ons from nowhere

- Position shifts using slides

- Wider intervals using string skipping

In the intermediate bootcamp, the basics were built in Week Four, then expanded in Week Ten.

Let's recap the elements above with three revision licks.

In Example 1j, downstrokes begin the ascending strings, followed by hammer-ons. On the way down, strings are initiated with a hammer-on from nowhere and followed by pull-offs.

Parentheses indicate the notes that begin strings without a pick stroke.

Example 1j:

The toughest part about sliding into higher and lower positions is not letting it affect your timing.

This A Minor scale lick has an abundance of ascending fourth finger slides and descending first finger slides, making it a good test of your position-shifting skills.

Example 1k:

For string skipping revision, here's a lick that can be treated as an Am11 arpeggio, but the notes also belong to the A Minor Pentatonic scale.

Since you already know where to put the hammer-ons from nowhere, only the pick strokes have been indicated on the relevant strings.

Example 1l:

This would be a good time to revise two-handed tapping, since it's basically an extension of legato using extra hammer-ons and pull-offs from fingers of the picking hand.

Like many of the techniques covered, the previous bootcamp divided tapping concepts into developmental drills (Week Eight) and more practical material (Week Thirteen).

We concluded the tapping chapters with vocabulary based on:

- Single-string sequences and etudes

- Diatonic and pentatonic scale usage

- Octave-jumping and string-skipping arpeggios

Here's a sequence to revise the way the hands work together in a descending "pedal point" sequence.

In each position, the tapping finger creates a pivot note that repeats between each lower note held by the fretting hand. The video for this example demonstrates what each position will look like.

Example 1m:

Instead of adding a tapping finger to extend your range beyond the fourth finger of the fretting hand, players like Reb Beach replace the fourth finger *with* the tapping finger. It creates a sound more akin to regular legato lines, since there aren't any wide intervals between the notes of each string.

In this lick, all fretting hand first finger notes are articulated with hammer-ons from nowhere. Rather than tapping from a fixed point, the two hands move in tandem.

Example 1n:

Moving a single-string D Minor triad shape across three octaves, Example 1o demonstrates one of the string-skipping tapping approaches covered in the intermediate bootcamp.

Example 1o:

In the practice plans for the new material in this book, we'll also revisit some concepts from *137 Guitar Speed & Coordination Exercises*, including the "speed burst" training approach undertaken in Week Seven of the intermediate bootcamp.

For now, let's look at this week's practice routine.

Week One Practice Plan

Most of the workouts in this book contain eight to ten examples, each played for a prescribed number of repeats and within selective speed zones (outlined in the Week Two plan).

Since this recap chapter contains fifteen licks and I still wish to stay within the thirty-minute format, this week's recommended practice routine will be a little different.

Days one and two of the plan will be time based – two minutes of repetition per lick, in free time. This will help in the cognitive stage of learning, focusing on hitting the right notes with the right timing.

To make interval practice easy, I recommend using a free Tabata app like *SmartWOD Timer* on your iPhone or Android device. This is an exercise app that allows you to program fixed intervals of work and rest as well as how many rounds in total.

Here's my recommended interval settings for days one and two. Begin each exercise slowly to absorb the details and accelerate through your repetitions until it's time to move on to the next drill.

For the remaining days of the week, warm up then choose the two most challenging drills from each technique in the recap to build a routine based on tempo training. I've created a sample routine in the table ahead.

Practice at three metronome speeds per drill, with each tempo far enough apart from the next to create a meaningful difference in how it feels to play.

Aim for the following in your tempo choices:

- Tempo 1: a comfortable speed at which you can execute any picking and fretting accurately

- Tempo 2: a moderate challenge while maintaining good form

- Tempo 3: the point where maintaining fast and accurate repeats is quite demanding

Small increments are often redundant because there isn't a significant enough challenge to your technique to evaluate your potential. Try 25-30 bpm increases, e.g., 120, 145, 170 bpm. If those jumps are too much, begin at a lower tempo or reduce the increment size.

Repeats full of mistakes don't count, so keep going until you have accurate reps.

Your three speeds might vary from day to day but should increase over time unless there's a fundamental problem to go back and address.

Here's a sample recap routine using drills from this chapter, with the number of repetitions and the total number of bars used.

Drill	Tempo 1 Reps	Tempo 2 Reps	Tempo 3 Reps
Warmup	Free time	-	-
Example 1b	3 x (12 bars total)	4 x (16 bars total)	4 x (16 bars total)
Example 1c	3 x (12 bars total)	4 x (16 bars total)	4 x (16 bars total)
Example 1e	3 x (12 bars total)	4 x (16 bars total)	4 x (16 bars total)
Example 1f	3 x (12 bars total)	4 x (16 bars total)	4 x (16 bars total)
Example 1h	3 x (12 bars total)	4 x (16 bars total)	4 x (16 bars total)
Example 1i	4 x (8 bars total)	4 x (8 bars total)	6 x (12 bars total)
Example 1k	3 x (12 bars total)	4 x (16 bars total)	4 x (16 bars total)
Example 1l	4 x (8 bars total)	4 x (8 bars total)	6 x (12 bars total)
Example 1n	4 x (8 bars total)	4 x (8 bars total)	6 x (12 bars total)
Example 1o	4 x (8 bars total)	4 x (8 bars total)	6 x (12 bars total)

The above routine will likely take less than thirty minutes, leaving you time to address any stumbling blocks with the selected examples or to throw in some of the drills you skipped.

Next week's routine provides an alternate picking focus using diatonic shred drills across all strings.

Week Two: Alternate Picking

This week's focus on alternate picking delivers a routine for keeping chops in good form, revitalising picking after a break, or developing new melodic sequences and lead-playing patterns.

The examples in this routine draw on scale fragments from the key of C Major or A Minor – often in three-note-per-string groups. Across the fretboard, the notes are laid out as follows:

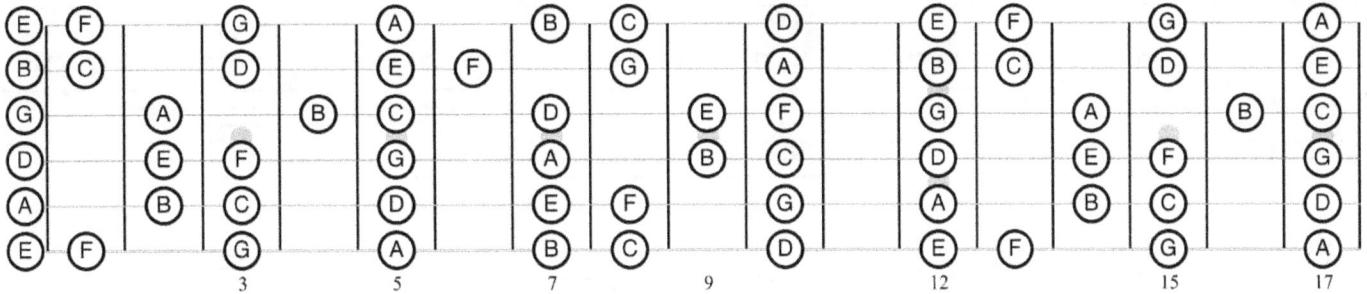

It will also be helpful to know the diatonic scales in seven, three-note-per-string patterns here, and in future chapters. We'll do a more detailed scale routine in Week Five.

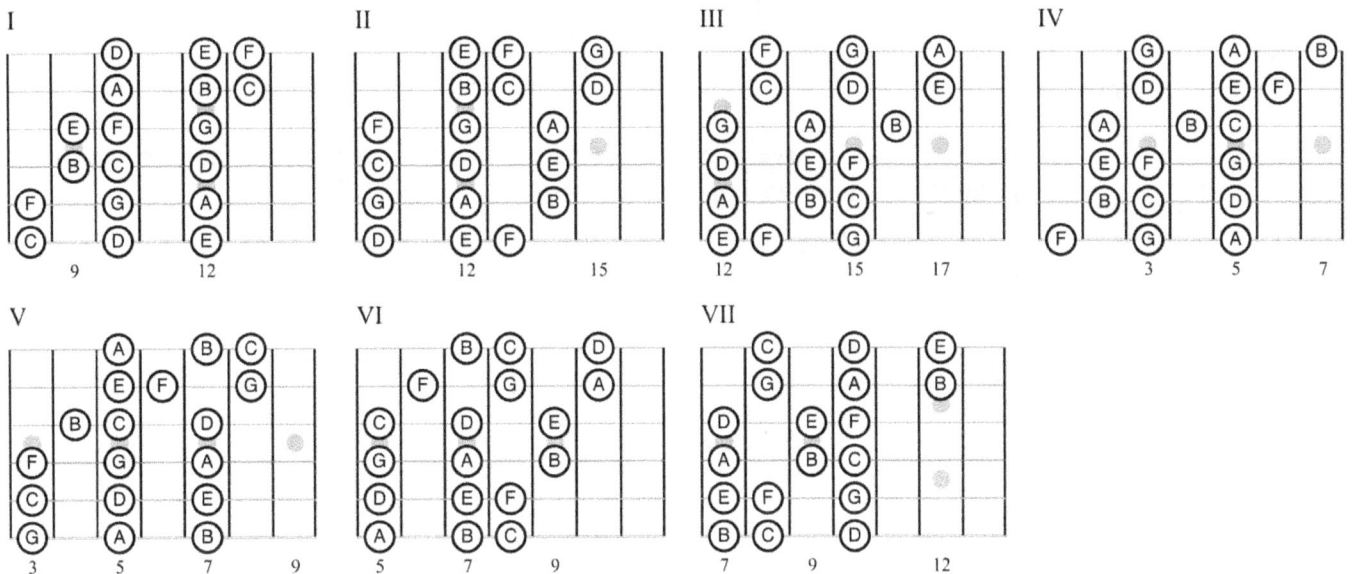

First up in the alternate picking routine is a one-bar pattern that is expanded to three octaves in subsequent bars.

A collection of motifs like this makes it handy to create a focus point or "practice cell" for the technique, with the ability to move it to other string groups for versatility and range.

For faster learning, focus on bar one until you understand the melodic pattern, then transfer it to the lower octaves in bars two and three.

As you can tell from the first run-through, this is an upstroke escape drill throughout.

Example 2a:

The next drill is another upstroke-escape sequence and one-bar melodic pattern, but there are no breaks between octave jumps this time. There's also a shift-slide on the highest string of each octave.

To make a seamless move to each lower octave, fret the last two notes in bars one and two with your fourth and second fingers, pre-empting the beginning of the next iteration.

Example 2b:

Any idea worth practicing is also worth reversing, so here are the concepts from the previous drill played in an ascending sequence.

This time, the position shift takes place on the lowest string of each octave with the general melodic idea of the previous drill played in reverse.

Example 2c:

Let's switch over to some downstroke-escape picking for the following three licks.

Beginning with three notes and following up with even numbers of notes per string keeps this two-bar motif in downward escape territory throughout.

The notes on each string are played melodically in various orders, so pay close attention to what's happening on each string before you move the "cell" up an octave in bars three and four.

Example 2d:

Example 2e is a downstroke escape version of Example 2b. Played one scale shape lower and with a note missing from the beginning of the latter sequence, this run is best studied as isolated bars at first, then connected for repetition practice.

Example 2e:

Containing mostly whole-tone stretches and a fourth finger slide in each octave, our last downward-escape drill has a little more work for the fretting hand to do than previous examples in the routine.

Example 2f:

Now that you've isolated the individual picking escape approaches, the rest of the routine focuses on mixing trajectories.

Example 2g contains an equal abundance of outside- and inside-picked string changes. As we've done several times, the basic drill is outlined first (bars one and two), then moved up an octave.

Example 2g:

The next drill is a sequence built on diatonic 2nd and 3rd intervals to target outside picking directly.

In bar one and most of bar two, ascending 2nds are played down the scale. From the 5th fret A note on the low E string, we move in ascending 3rds up the scale.

Example 2h:

Removing a note from the previous run turns it into an exclusively inside-picked sequence.

Example 2i:

The final drill in this routine is designed to test picking accuracy, stamina, and speed. While also an excellent economy picking lick, too, the aim here is switching from outside to inside picking.

Example 2j:

Now that you've tested the material, let's look at how you'll practice this week.

Week Two Practice Plan

This week's practice will include learning time, tempo training, and speed bursts.

You can use every drill presented in the chapter or choose half now, half later. The essential things are to adopt effective, targeted practice and address the three escape paths of alternate picking.

Spend at least one practice session learning the drills in free time using the Tabata method, then begin tempo training in the next session.

Choose speeds for your tempo training that reflect what you can manage while creating challenges. In other words, please don't make it all too easy or too far out of reach.

As well as the three-speed approach to metronome work, I recommend some time spent pushing your max speed with free time practice and speed-burst training.

Below, drills are to be played three times at each of your selected metronome speeds. Then, turn off the click or drum beat and try blasting each drill a few times at your top speed, putting some space between repeats to give your muscles a chance to relax and go again.

Tempos one to three should be performed accurately, but "max speed" repeats don't have to be perfect. This final process aims to raise the ceiling of your speed a little more with each practice session.

Playing only to a metronome might be holding you back, so the idea is to let the dog off the leash in the fourth stage of each example after you've done the disciplined work.

Drill	Tempo 1 Reps	Tempo 2 Reps	Tempo 3 Reps	Max Speed Reps
Warmup	Free time	-	-	-
Examples 2a – 2j	3 x (12 bars)	3 x (12 bars)	3 x (12 bars)	3 x (12 bars)

Supercharge your speed with "Burst Training"

The other approach for speed maximisation is "burst training" using modified versions of selected drills. You can add this modification to any practice session, be it daily or later in the week.

Adding spaces to some previous material and playing it in high-speed bursts can expose you to speeds beyond your current limits with the steady, regular versions.

Here's a modification of Example 2a for you to consider. I've performed it in the bonus video content to get you in the frame of mind for pushing boundaries. See how you can apply this modification concept to other drills in the routine.

Example 2k:

Creating a burst version of Example 2d, here's a variation separating the drill's ascending and descending portions.

Example 2l:

If you want to include some revision material from last week, do so at the end of the routine so that your main practice time is used on the primary goal.

In summary, your practice this week will include:

- Learning time – one to two days as needed

- Tempo training – remaining days of the practice week

- Max speed repetitions – for each drill after metronome work

- Speed burst variations – add to selected days of your choice

- Revision – choose some drills from last week to complement any session if you have time.

We'll focus on the fretting hand in the next routine with some new legato work.

Week Three: Legato

This week, we'll run through nine legato sequences that incorporate hammer-ons, pull-offs, slides, string-skips, and initiating strings with pick strokes and hammer-ons from nowhere.

All of the diatonic sequences are in the key of G Major. For each lick, I've suggested an accompanying chord, but feel free to try any of the patterns over any G Major or E Minor chord progressions.

When I mention specific scale patterns, I'm referring to the seven shapes mapped out at the beginning of Week Two.

See Routine Three of the *Guitar Practice Warmup Routines* book to get your fretting hand warmed up for legato work.

The first drill in the routine is a chromatic run played in two octaves, using every finger. It's a good one for rhythmic focus, so adhere to a strict 1/16th note rhythm until the sextuplets in bars two and four.

To remind you to initiate descending strings with fourth finger hammer-ons from nowhere, relevant notes are in parentheses. In future examples, these will be omitted unless necessary.

Example 3a:

Using the fourth three-note-per-string scale pattern in the key of G Major, Example 3b zig-zags in a general upward direction in bars one and two, with a descending counterpoint in bars three and four.

Like all the positional sequences, this run can be transposed to any other scale shape in the key for extra fretboard coverage.

Example 3b:

Applying string skipping to a couple of minor-tonality patterns, the following sequence uses odd numbers of notes per string, such as threes, fives, and sevens. Since the rhythm is built on 1/16th notes, be sure to maintain good timing.

While both halves of the sequence are played over minor 7th chords, the scale shapes vary slightly to remain in the key of G Major.

Example 3c:

Since many legato runs begin strings with either the first or fourth fingers, we can target the other digits in sequences like Example 3d.

After beginning on the first string, this lick initiates subsequent strings using hammer-ons from nowhere with the second and third fingers (as indicated). Shifting positions at the end of bar three, the sequence descends similarly.

Hammer-ons from nowhere still apply regardless of direction for the zig-zagging string skipping portions.

Example 3d:

Example 3e is a speedy position-shifting loop played in three octaves. Each main bar can be played as many times as you like before jumping to the next octave. The sequence ends with a tap, which can be done using the index or second fingers of the picking hand, according to preference.

Example 3e:

Arpeggios can be laid out in a way that is legato-playing friendly, too. Here, diatonic seventh arpeggios from the key of G Major are arranged two notes per string, with the 7th degree as the lowest chord tone in each shape.

Using the idea of arpeggio-stacking, I play these arpeggios in diatonic 3rds through the key over a static chord.

At high speeds, the rhythm creates a "burst" feel in the styles of Joe Satriani and Steve Vai.

Example 3f:

Calling on four-note-per-string scales, this sequence uses three fingers and a position shift on each string to venture from the 3rd fret of the sixth string to the 19th fret of the first string.

Example 3g:

Example 3h is a counterpart to the previous sequence, travelling down a four-note-per-string pattern that is a diatonic shift down from the last shape.

As with any sequence involving position slides, it's imperative that you stick to the rhythm unless deliberately going for a loose time feel.

Example 3h:

Our final sequence in this routine combines the second major scale shape from the key of G Major with chromatic passing tones.

Unlike previous sequences, I use pick strokes on lower strings in this legato line, since there's only one note each time the lick doubles back to an earlier string.

At speed, this conjures up the sounds of Brett Garsed and Greg Howe.

Example 3i:

Let's take a look at the practice plan for this material.

Week Three Practice Plan

Our targeted areas for legato are technique, timing, and flow. Find the optimum amount of finger pressure and avoid being too aggressive with hammer-ons and pull-offs. Aim for graceful execution and you'll be better positioned to speed up.

This week's routine comprises nine drills of four bars each. As usual, your first day or two is learning time. Don't push yourself on these days. Instead, do your best to absorb the melodic idea behind each sequence and look out for any mechanical snags like slides or jumps between strings.

Warm up before this routine using Routine Three from the "Warmups" book or with some slow and accurate repetitions of Example 3a from this chapter.

If you're still building your endurance as a legato player, shake off any tension and take a few bars to rest between repeats if you need to.

To ensure your picking chops don't fall by the wayside while focusing on the fretting hand, the program below includes revision examples of each alternate picking approach from the previous week.

A short mix of high/medium tempo and "max speed" repetitions should be sufficient for any revision work.

Tempo training days will look like this:

Drill	Tempo 1 Reps	Tempo 2 Reps	Tempo 3 Reps	Max Speed Reps
Warmup	Free time	-	-	-
Examples 3a – 3i	3 x (12 bars)	3 x (12 bars)	3 x (12 bars)	3 x (12 bars)
Example 2b	-	4 x (16 bars)	-	4 x (16 bars)
Example 2e	-	4 x (16 bars)	-	4 x (16 bars)
Example 2i	-	4 x (16 bars)	-	4 x (16 bars)

As a bonus burst-training example to push your general legato speed, here's an excerpt from Example 3c with some strategic rests.

Example 3j:

Next, we'll harness the powers of directional motion in a new economy-picking routine.

Week Four: Economy Picking

In this economy-picking practice routine, you'll be honing your string-changing skills with a range of sequences that move vertically and horizontally on the fretboard, as well as turnaround strategies and various numbers of notes per string (primarily odds).

First, let's wake up your sweep-picking string changes with a chromatic ascending and descending run.

This drill makes an excellent warmup for economy picking, which will be its main role in the routine. Ensure that every doubled downstroke and upstroke snaps to the new string without a separate motion in between.

Example 4a:

Moving to diatonic sequences in the key of C Major, Example 4b is a two-bar sequence played in four places. Bars five to eight are the same notes, an octave lower than the first four bars.

Only one string change per line is picked without a sweeping motion, using two inside-picking strokes. The "two-stroke turnaround" occurs in the first bar of each line, from the highest string back to the next string down.

Example 4b:

Measures 5-6 (TAB):

```
5
-------------------------------------------7---------------7--9--10-
-------------------7--9--10---10--9--7------------------7--9--10------
---------7--8--10-----------------------10--8--7--------7--8--10------
--7--8--10-----------------------------------------10--7--8--10-------
6
```

Measures 7-8 (TAB):

```
7
--------------------------------9-----------------------9--10--12-
------------------9--10--12--12--10--9------------9--10--12--------
--------8--10--12-----------------------12--10--8-----8--10--12----
--8--10--12-------------------------------------12--8--10--12------
8
```

The next run is a four-string position-shifting sequence that mixes three- and five notes per string in each bar until sliding to the next position. You can extend the idea by ascending and descending as many times as you like, or by moving it to any other four-string group in the key.

Example 4c:

Bars 1-2 (TAB):

```
1
                                    5--8--5--7--8---10--8--7-
                       5--6--8----------------------10--6--10--8--6-
         4--7--4--5--7-----------------------------------------9--7--5-
--3--5--7------------------------------------------------9--5--9--7--5-
∏ V ∏ ∏ V ∏ V ∏ ∏ V ∏ ∏ V ∏ V ∏    V ∏ V V ∏ V ∏ V V ∏ V V ∏ V ∏ V
2
```

Bars 3-4 (TAB):

```
3
                                     8--12--8--10--12--13--12--10-
                        8--10--12------------------------13--10--13--12--10-
           7--10--7--9--10--------------------------------------------12--10--9-
--7--9--10-------------------------------------------------------------------
∏ V ∏ ∏ V ∏ V ∏ ∏ V ∏ ∏ V ∏ V ∏    V ∏ V V ∏ V ∏ V V ∏ V
4
```

It's time to work horizontally, moving up the fretboard in string pairs. Each section of this lick begins in the 3rd position, adhering to the notes in the key on each string.

Besides being a focused picking drill, it's also a handy tool for position shifting anytime you want to get out of a scale shape and into another area of the fretboard.

Example 4d:

The eight notes that begin Example 4e make up a turnaround lick that reappears in lower octaves from the 7th fret of the fourth string to the 5th fret of the sixth string. Descending scale notes connect these fragments. In bar four, the sequence repeats one diatonic position higher.

Example 4e:

We can use the same idea when going up the scale, even turning it into another horizontal lick, as shown here along the second and first strings.

Example 4f:

A few melodic ideas are going on in the next lick, but the most crucial part is to take this mish-mash of three-, four-, five-, and six-note motifs and play it as consistent 1/16th notes. It's crucial to avoid any mindset in which playing three notes on a string makes something a triplet or that five notes equate to odd tuplets.

Bars one and two contain thematic repetitions of a descending three-string motif, while the last two bars use six-note groups to move up the second and first strings.

Example 4g:

The last two examples in this routine are slightly more complex than the "raw speed" kind of licks, as they break out of the three-note-per-string routine with alternating single-note inclusions.

Perfect for playing over ii and vi chords from the key, Example 4h uses single notes on the sixth, fourth, and second strings in both directions.

The exact shape used in the first two bars is repeated from the 10th fret of the sixth string in bars three and four.

Example 4h:

The last sequence combines the diatonic scale (the D Dorian mode of C Major), a creative three-note-per-string D Minor Pentatonic sequence, and an Fmaj7 arpeggio.

This example is the most complex of the book thus far, so take your time to work through each bar to absorb its contents before applying speed.

Example 4i:

Week Four Practice Plan

The material in this economy picking routine contains a mixed bag of mechanical and musical applications, so you might prefer to focus on the first five or six drills as technique practice, then add the others later.

Remember that the aim is to use this week to get better at economy picking, develop freedom with the technique, and to use my drills to achieve those bigger goals. When a drill is no longer serving that purpose, that's the time to replace it with a new challenge.

On the first day of the week, run through examples 4a to 4f without the metronome. This is the time to get the notes right and focus on smooth execution.

On day two, use Example 4a as the warmup drill and examples 4b to 4f for tempo training. Complete the routine with a legato and alternate picking drill of your choice for revision (samples offered below).

Drill	Tempo 1 Reps	Tempo 2 Reps	Tempo 3 Reps	Max Speed Reps
Example 4a	Warmup	-	-	-
Examples 4b – 4f	3 x	3 x	3 x	3 x
Example 3c	-	4 x	-	4 x
Example 2j	-	4 x	-	4 x

After a few days, learn the remaining economy picking examples and modify your tempo plan to the following:

Drill	Tempo 1 Reps	Tempo 2 Reps	Tempo 3 Reps	Max Speed Reps
Example 4a	Warmup	-	-	-
Examples 4b – 4f	-	3 x	3 x	3 x
Examples 4g – 4i	4 x	4 x	4 x	4 x

If economy picking doesn't feel intuitive to you as a player, I recommend spending some extra time noodling in free time, improvising with your fretting hand while trying to adhere to the principles of economy picking with your picking hand.

Start with simple phrases and work up to spontaneous application of the runs in this chapter.

The more practical time you spend on the technique, the bigger your chances of harnessing its strengths more naturally, rather than having it remain an academic exercise.

Week Five: Scale Routine

Having covered the "big three" of scale playing techniques (alternate picking, legato, economy picking), now would be a perfect time to check in on your fretboard knowledge and look at some ways of practicing scales.

While the lion's share of rock guitarists work from the three-notes-per-string playbook, we can put some great twists on that format to open up the fretboard and break out of scale jail.

First, let's connect those three-note patterns at the top and bottom to ensure you know them. Here are the seven patterns in the key of G Major, beginning from the F# note on the sixth string.

You can run this drill using any picking type or legato (better still, all three!)

Example 5a:

Next, shift positions on different strings and in less predictable places, staying in the key of G Major. I like to use economy picking for this one, but take your pick of techniques.

Example 5b:

The next run travels a longer path between two G notes on the 15th fret of the first string and the 3rd fret of the sixth string.

It's also a great candidate for economy picking, so I'll suggest the pick strokes that move to each string most efficiently.

Example 5c:

Four-note-per-string scales are an instant box-breaker, so I recommend learning to navigate them.

Example 5d uses a format that we'll adapt over the following few examples, so take a good look at this G Major option.

Bars one to three use the same ascending motif on each string, adjusting for the key each time. In bar three, a descending version begins one diatonic position higher. We used a similar sequence as a legato line in Example 3h.

Example 5d:

To play the previous lick in any key, we don't necessarily have to move the whole pattern to a far-away fret and begin learning it elsewhere.

Instead, we can adjust the pattern to suit another key and take advantage of the same fretboard span. This requires knowing what sharps and flats belong to each key – a worthwhile piece of knowledge.

To play in the key of C Major, lower all the F# notes from the last run to make them F natural. Every other note in the sequence stays the same.

Example 5e:

```
1                                         2
                                    7—9—10—12—10—9—10—12
                          5—7—9—10—9—7—9—10
              3—5—7—8—7—5—7—8
1—3—5—7—5—3—5—7
```

```
3                                         4
                    12—13—15—17—15—13—15—17    19—17—15—13—15—17—15—13
10—12—13—15—13—12—13—15                                    17—15—13—12—13—15—13—12
```

```
5                                         6
14—12—10—9—10—12—10—9
            12—10—9—7—9—10—9—7
                        10—8—7—5—7—8—7—5
                                    8—7—5—3—5—7—5—3
```

By knowing the notes in other keys, you can modify the above form to suit any key.

For example, to play it in the key of F Major, lower all the B natural notes a semitone to Bb. For the key of D Major, start with all the natural notes, then sharpen all the F and C notes. See the list at the end of this section (before the practice plan) as a reference for other keys.

Let's change the scale type now from C Major (Example 5e) to A Harmonic Minor (A, B, C, D, E, F, G#), raising any G natural notes by a semitone.

This run sounds excellent over the V chord of A Harmonic Minor, so try it with an E7 chord.

Example 5f:

Since diatonic scales contain seven notes, we can use combinations of four- and three-notes-per-string to complete one octave of a scale on two strings. This means that other octaves can use the same shapes.

Here's the A Dorian mode (A, B, C, D, E, F#, G) from the key of G Major. I use separate fingers (instead of slides) for each four-note row in this particular shape.

On the way down, a different shape is used, including sliding position shifts.

For the execution, I use economy picking on the way up, then alternate picking and pull-offs on the way down. This is the approach often taken in my book, *Neoclassical Speed Strategies for Guitar*, which uses the Yngwie Malmsteen picking system.

Example 5g:

Executed with the same picking system, here's the A Mixolydian mode (A, B, C#, D, E, F#, G) from the key of D Major. This drill uses a single shape up and down the scale.

Example 5h:

To complete this routine, let's compare three-note-per-string forms to combinations of four and three.

Here's an A Melodic Minor scale (A, B, C, D, E, F#, G#) played from the 7th degree.

In bar three, beat 2, the pattern switches to four notes on the sixth, fourth, and second strings, venturing up to the 14th fret F# note by the end of the shape.

In practice time, see what other scales you can use this "side-by-side" approach with.

Example 5i:

To alter the key of Example 5e from C Major to other keys, apply the changes below.

Sharps

C major / A minor	(none)
G major / E minor	F♯
D major / B minor	F♯, C♯
A major / F-sharp minor	F♯, C♯, G♯
E major / C-sharp minor	F♯, C♯, G♯, D♯
B major / G-sharp minor	F♯, C♯, G♯, D♯, A♯
F-sharp major / D-sharp minor	F♯, C♯, G♯, D♯, A♯, E♯
C-sharp major / A-sharp minor	F♯, C♯, G♯, D♯, A♯, E♯, B♯

Flats

C major / A minor	(none)
F major / D minor	B♭
B-flat major / G minor	B♭, E♭
E-flat major / C minor	B♭, E♭, A♭
A-flat major / F minor	B♭, E♭, A♭, D♭
D-flat major / B-flat minor	B♭, E♭, A♭, D♭, G♭
G-flat major / E-flat minor	B♭, E♭, A♭, D♭, G♭, C♭
C-flat major / A-flat minor	B♭, E♭, A♭, D♭, G♭, C♭, F♭

Week Five Practice Plan

This routine contains six concepts explored across nine examples. The concepts are:

1. Joining three-note-per-string patterns at the top and bottom

2. Joining three-note-per-string patterns at various points and strings

3. Four-note-per-string scale coverage

4. Modifying four-note-per-string patterns for other keys

5. Alternating four- and three-note-per-string layouts

6. Comparing three-note-per-string layouts to the four-plus-three layout

Rather than focusing on repetition via tempo training this week, I recommend including the following approaches in your scale practice:

- Executing the scales with solid timing, controlled attack, and various techniques

- Coming up with your favourite position-shifting licks and patterns

- Adjusting the patterns in the routine to suit other keys and tonalities

- Looking at what other scales you can arrange in formats like four-notes-per-string, alternating fours and threes, etc.

Since you probably won't need to repeat scales for the entirety of your practice sessions this week, revise by incorporating two examples from weeks two, three, and four in your regimen.

In the next routine, we'll delve deeper into sweep-picked arpeggio practice.

Week Six: Sweep Picking Arpeggios

This sweep-picking arpeggio routine advances the technique beyond our last look, with more demanding picking patterns and a wider variety of shapes.

Since this material cuts to the chase without much ado, so shall I!

Example 6a, in the key of F Major, compares five-string and six-string triad shapes and changes directions with doubled notes (bars one and three) and single notes (sixth string, bars two and four). The triad shape is our familiar extension of the "C shape" from the CAGED system.

You might be tempted to play this drill rhythmically as 1/16th note triplets, but stay with the written rhythm since that's part of the control factor of the lick.

Example 6a:

Now that your sweeping is warmed up, let's try a variety of triad types that crawl down the fretboard.

Playing triads in the order shown (major, minor, diminished) lowers one note by a semitone each time, leading us to eventually change the root note and move down the fretboard as far as we want.

Here are the three triad shapes repeated in Example 6b, along with the fingers used to fret them:

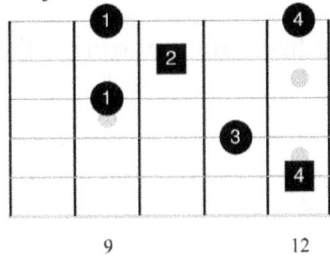

Major

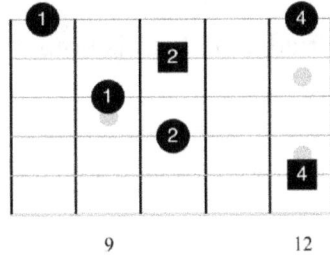

Minor

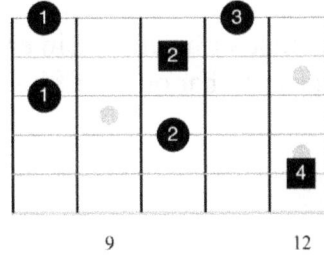

Diminished

Example 6b:

Playing through a chord progression from the key of F Major, the next drill uses major and minor triads.

Rather than sweep-pick the first string change in each triad, a pull-off is used on the first string, mirroring the hammer-on halfway through each bar on the fifth string.

Example 6c:

Upping the ante with exclusive single-note direction changes, Example 6d comprises longer motifs for each triad with more turnarounds and six beats per bar.

This chord progression moves from the key of D Minor (bars one and two) to C Minor, though both keys contain the Bb chord.

Example 6d:

It's time to look at some odd-tuplet groupings with three- and four-string sweeps.

Using the chord progression from the classic *Canon* by Johann Pachelbel (1653-1706), examples 6e and 6f break out of the rhythmic conventions of playing arpeggios in threes and fours. It will also have you jumping around the fretboard quite a bit.

Fitting the notes of each three-string triad into seven 1/16th notes per beat, the first of these smaller picking patterns requires some adept direction changing and adherence to beginning each new triad on the beat.

The best approach for learning it is to play in free time, then introduce a slow beat to lock in with at the beginning of each triad.

Example 6e:

Extending the previous sweeps by one string gives us nine notes per triad. I play these in alternating 1/16th note and quintuplet (five 1/16th notes per beat) groups. Some floating around rhythmically is to be expected with an unorthodox rhythm, but aim to start each new triad at the right time.

Example 6f:

The next example introduces shapes taught in my book, *Sweep Picking Speed Strategies for Guitar*.

We've already used the extended C chord form for major and minor triads. Let's see it with the two other shapes, based on the CAGED chord shapes of E and A Major, plus their minor forms.

Each dot is labelled by chord tones, with fingerings suggested in the notation of Example 6g:

Here's a drill that moves through the major and minor shapes beginning on the root notes (bars one to four), 3rds (bars five to eight), and 5ths (bars nine to twelve).

Example 6g:

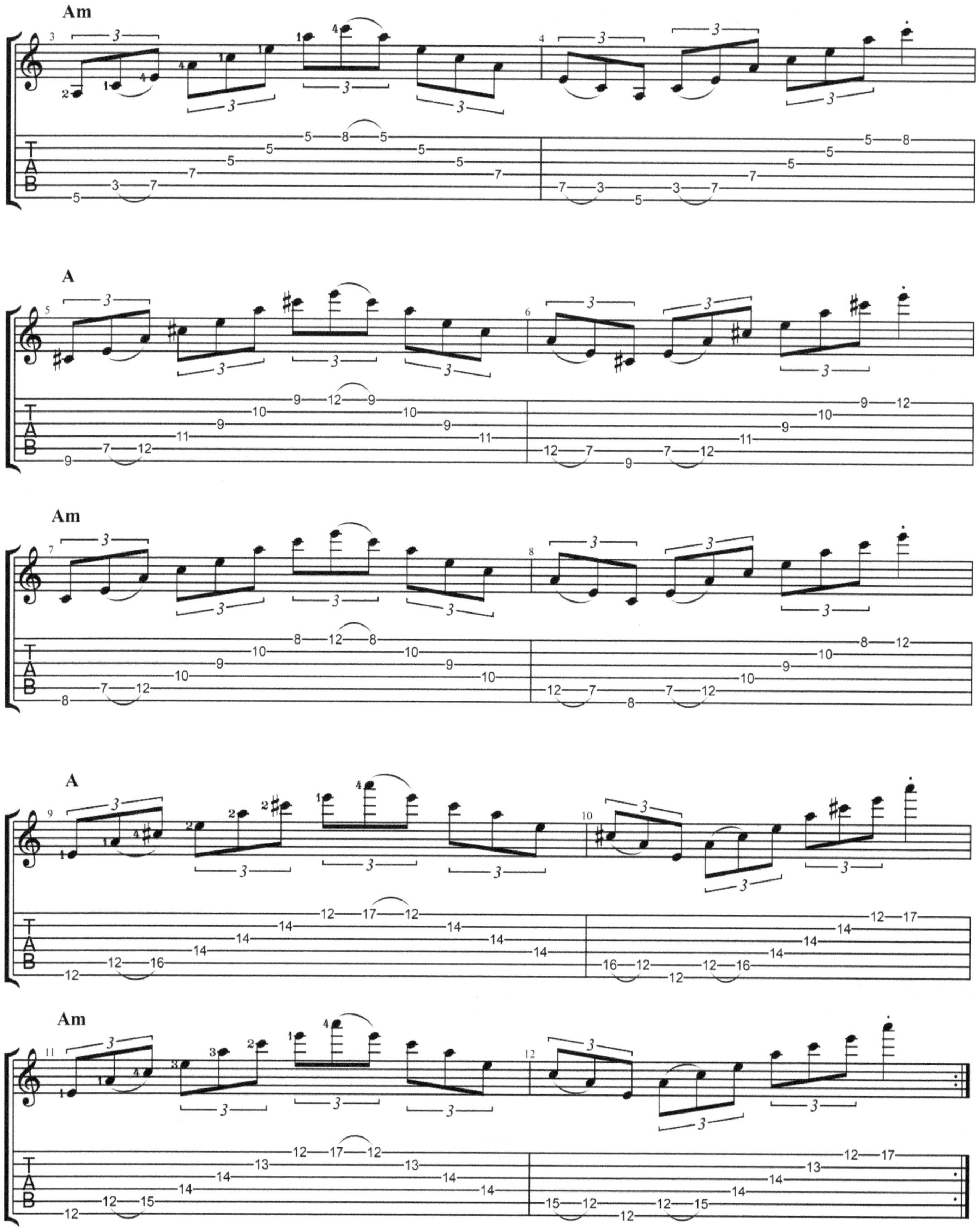
Am
A
Am
A
Am
TAB

Calling on a mix of major triad shapes, here's an etude written in the style of Jason Becker.

This piece requires attention to detail in your articulation to achieve a high level of performance, so keep an eye on every note, finger-roll, and pick stroke to ensure it's clean, accurate, and in-time.

For the more adventurous among you, it can also be played as a minor triad etude by substituting triad shapes for each chord.

Example 6h:

For the final drill in this routine, we'll venture into seventh chords from a root note of C, changing one note each time to work through major 7th, dominant 7th, minor 7th, half-diminished (m7b5), and diminished 7th chords.

Cmaj7   C7   Cm7

Cm7b5   Cdim7

Example 6i:

Cmaj7

C7

Cm7

Cm7♭5

Cdim7

Week Six Practice Plan

This is another week in which the material can be split into separate practice sessions or spread across multiple weeks, depending on your previous experience.

I suggest a learning day, for examples 6a to 6f, followed by tempo training days to push your technique. If you're a budding Becker or Gambale already and want to go all-in, you might like to alternate between the two sweep-picking programs below.

Because timing is such a crucial aspect of sweep picking, we'll retire "Max Speed" free time repetitions for this week, but for selected examples, try pushing into a fourth round of tempo work.

Although this book is formatted into a thirteen-week plan to cover many bases in just a few months, advanced sweep picking can take several more weeks or months to come to fruition. So, take on what you can (or a little more), and add extra material as you progress.

Technique Builder

Drill	Tempo 1 Reps	Tempo 2 Reps	Tempo 3 Reps	Tempo 4 Reps
Example 6a	3 x (12 bars)	3 x (12 bars)	3 x (12 bars)	2 x (8 bars)
Example 6b	1 x (12 bars)	1 x (12 bars)	1 x (12 bars)	-
Example 6c	3 x (12 bars)	3 x (12 bars)	3 x (12 bars)	2 x (8 bars)
Example 6d	3 x (12 bars)	3 x (12 bars)	3 x (12 bars)	-
Example 6e	4 x (8 bars)	4 x (8 bars)	4 x (8 bars)	2 x (8 bars)
Example 6f	3 x (12 bars)	3 x (12 bars)	3 x (12 bars)	-
Example 6g	Learning mode	-	-	-

Vocabulary Builder

Drill	Tempo 1 Reps	Tempo 2 Reps	Tempo 3 Reps
Example 6g	2 x (24 bars)	2 x (24 bars)	2 x (24 bars)
Example 6h	2 x (16 bars)	2 x (16 bars)	2 x (16 bars)
Example 6i	3 x (15 bars)	3 x (15 bars)	3 x (15 bars)

Scale Revision with various techniques

Drill	Tempo 1 Reps	Tempo 2 Reps
Example 5c	2 x (8 bars)	2 x (8 bars)
Example 5e	2 x (12 bars)	2 x (12 bars)
Example 5i	2 x (8 bars)	2 x (8 bars)

Week Seven: Maintenance Program

So far, we've added a new technique each week, constructed a practice routine, and allocated a little time at the end for revision. This is a valuable way to build new skills using "targeted practice", allowing new material to become a focal point of your work in its developmental stages.

Another essential practice format is the maintenance program, or "comprehensive practice", in which existing topics are revised, improved, accelerated, etc – like a full-body workout for your guitar.

Instead of working on one subject, comprehensive practice sessions address several areas of playing in one sitting, keeping your chops in good form, and preventing ideas from falling by the wayside.

Planning is the most critical part of any practice session, so choosing a format, the content, and the time allocation, are all steps to getting the best value for your time. Practicing aimlessly might begin with the best of intentions but end up leaving you feeling disappointed if you didn't get to work on everything you wanted to.

Using subjects covered in the book, we'll explore three formats for you to consider for technique maintenance and versatility. The formats are:

- Pie chart practice (time allocation)

- Circuit training

- Modified practice

Pie-chart practice allocates a fixed time to a chosen range of subjects. When the clock reaches a predetermined time limit, you move on, no matter what. At the end of a time-based practice session, you'll feel a sense of accomplishment from sticking to your guns and managing your time well.

Allocating time for a warmup, then alternate picking, legato, sweep picking, and economy picking, might divide an hour of practice time like this:

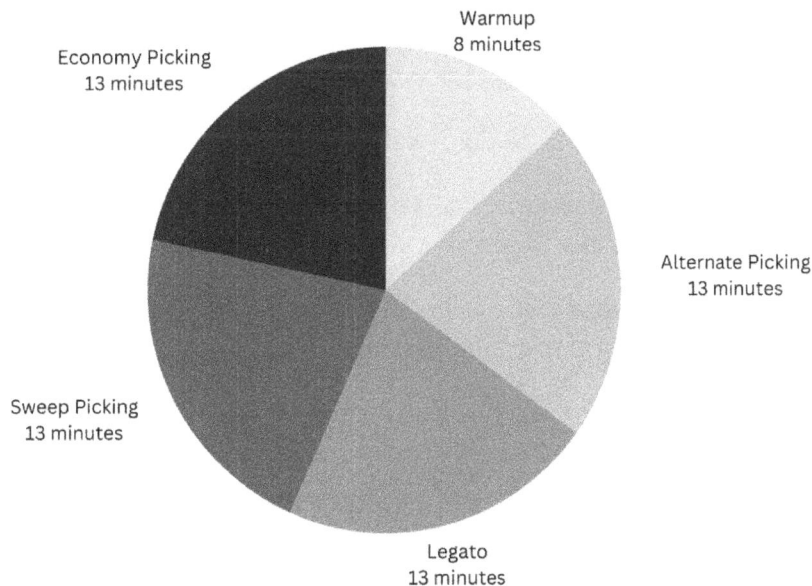

Warmup
8 minutes

Alternate Picking
13 minutes

Legato
13 minutes

Sweep Picking
13 minutes

Economy Picking
13 minutes

Each segment of the pie works like a mini-workout. In this case, you might fill it with:

- Warmup: five drills from *Guitar Practice Warmup Routines*

- Alternate Picking: six drills from Week Two, played for two minutes each

- Legato: six drills from Week Three, two minutes each

- Sweep Picking: six drills from Week Six, two minutes each

- Economy Picking: six drills from Week Four, two minutes each

Choose from tempo-, free-time, or burst-training and allow a 1-minute break between techniques to make one hour.

Alternatively, with the three-speed metronome approach, you could choose fewer drills and spend more time on each. Four drills at a minute per tempo gives you twelve minutes.

Circuit Training is another time-based workout format, but instead of practicing each technique in larger blocks, a selected number of drills of all types are played in shorter intervals, then repeated from the beginning.

Here's an example of a circuit played three times. A Tabata app will be perfect for keeping track here.

- Round One: two exercises from alternate picking, legato, sweep picking, and economy picking, played for 90 seconds each with a 20-second break – warmup level

- Round Two: repeat the same drills at a higher tempo (medium intensity), either with a metronome or setting your own pace. 90 seconds of work with 20-second breaks

- Round Three: high-intensity round, doing as many reps of each drill as possible in 90 seconds with breaks

The above circuit training session comes in at forty-four minutes at three rounds. With one drill per subject, it will be twenty-two minutes.

This format is excellent for gradually dialling up the difficulty of your practice as you go.

The final practice format I'd like you to consider is called **Modified Practice**.

In this mode, the aim is to adapt your favourite drills by playing them on different strings, or in different keys/tonalities, extending ideas in ways that will get you thinking differently.

As mentioned in the *137 Guitar Speed & Coordination Exercises* book, there's some science behind using variations and permutations to improve your technique.

According to a study by researchers for the John Hopkins University School of Medicine, altering tasks during repetition-based practice sessions may reduce the time required to master a skill, compared to repeating it the same way every time.

In the study, eighty-six volunteers were assigned a computer-based motor skill to learn. The participants who used a modified practice routine performed better in the second test than in the first.

The results supported the notion of *reconsolidation*, where memories are recalled and augmented with new information to improve motor skills.

According to the study's senior author, Dr. Pablo Celnik, "If you practice a slightly modified version of a task you want to master, you learn more and faster than if you just keep practicing the same thing multiple times in a row."

"Our results are important because little was known before about how reconsolidation works in relation to motor skill development. This shows how simple manipulations during training can lead to more rapid and larger motor skill gains because of reconsolidation," says Celnik. "The goal is to develop training schedules that give people more improvement for the same amount of practice time." (Source: *Current Biology* journal, January 28, 2016).

To create effective practice routines after studying the prescribed plans in the book, consider reducing the number of tasks per session and increasing the number of variations used, focusing on the areas that challenge you the most.

To demonstrate, here are some variations to try.

This drill retools the basic motif behind Example 1a from the Week Two alternate picking routine. The rhythm has been changed to sextuples, the melodic pattern is now an A Harmonic Minor line, and the phrasing has no pauses.

Example 7a:

Based on Example 2b, the next alternate picking lick expands the single-string sequences on the first, third, and fifth strings.

Extending the idea like this is good for stamina and also some single-string picking focus.

Example 7b:

Recommended as a free-time practice example, this sweep-picking arpeggio sequence combines the string-changing moves from examples 6e, 6f, and 6e from last week's routine.

Example 7c:

A quirky mix of time signatures, this modified economy picking drill is based on Example 4e.

The turnaround figure used at three points in the original lick has been expanded with a position shift up and back on the second and first strings (bar one) and on the fourth and third strings (bar three).

Example 7d:

In legato land, this modification of 3e (middle and higher octaves) spends more time on each string pair by moving the lick up one diatonic position before moving up to the next octave.

The one-bar phrase behind the lick therefore gets more work in this modded phrase.

Example 7e:

Next up, two six-string A Major triad shapes from Example 6g have been combined. The rhythm has changed from 1/8th note triplets to 1/16th notes, and the two-bar phrase is then transposed to a C Major triad in bars three and four.

The shapes now require you to think in rhythmic groups of four and also to play them in two keys.

Example 7f:

Demonstrating exaggeration in modification exercises, here's a side-by-side of the adjacent string changes in Example 1c, made more difficult with string skipping in bar two.

Example 7g:

Your mission for practice this week is to try each of the formats presented, creating a revision plan from material that has challenged you in the past week.

Try alternating between the pie chart and circuit training approaches for most of the week, then work through my modifications of past drills in this chapter to get a feel for the process. Compare regular versions of the drills with suggested modifications in this chapter and come up with your own.

In weeks nine and ten, we'll add two new routines to the roster, introducing hybrid picking in Week Eight and revisiting two-handed tapping in Week Nine.

Week Eight: Hybrid Picking

Hybrid picking is so named because it combines the pick (held between thumb and first finger) and plucking from one or more fingers of the picking hand.

The contrast between pick attack and finger tone makes hybrid picking another great tool to have at your disposal.

If you haven't done fingerpicking before, the Week Seven chapter of *Guitar Practice Warmup Routines* is a good place to start. That said, the drills below build progressively and will work as technique builders if you start at a comfortable pace.

This routine includes nine drills, beginning with a basic primer that alternates between downstrokes of the pick and plucking from fingers two and three (Example 8a).

A "pop" indicator is included alongside the pick strokes to show where the finger picking occurs, accompanied by either "m" (medio) or "a" (annular) in the notation to specify the second or third fingers of the picking hand, respectively.

The notes in this drill will be played separately, i.e., not overlapping.

Example 8a:

Next, we'll arpeggiate triads using a "forward roll" of downstroke-medio-annular repetitions and separated notes.

The chord progression is the i, iv, and v chords in the key of A Minor, followed by I, IV, and V chords from the relative key of C Major.

Example 8b:

Here's a "backward roll" picked with the third finger, second finger, and a downstroke with repetitions.

Since the notes ring in this example, a clean(ish) guitar tone works best.

Example 8c:

Moving to scale-based ideas, Example 8d uses an A Minor Pentatonic box, picking one note per string and hammering another note on each.

Three-string groups are created from the sixth string in bar one and the fifth string in bar three.

Example 8d:

Using the A Minor and D Minor Pentatonic scales, we'll execute the next sequence using the pick, middle finger, hammer-ons, and pull-offs.

Example 8e:

Hybrid picking has become a common tool of rock and fusion legato players thanks to the influence of Australia's Brett Garsed in the 1980s and '90s.

Here, we'll use plucking to initiate adjacent higher strings in a three-note-per-string A Minor scale sequence.

For fast string changes like these, I use my third finger for the plucking because of its similar length to the first finger. You're welcome to use the second finger if you're more comfortable with it.

Example 8f:

Sequencing in "descending fours" with the minor pentatonic scale results in two four-note picking patterns that alternate: pluck, pull-off, down, pull-off, and pluck, down, pull-off, down.

Example 8g:

With the full natural minor scale in descending fours, three picking patterns emerge in sequence, seen in each bar of the next lick.

Examples 8h:

Lastly, in the routine, we'll use "ascending fours" in a D Dorian-sounding sequence.

This introduces sweep picking into the hybrid picking skillset, with double downstrokes used in the third step of the sequence in bars one to three.

Example 8i:

Week Eight Practice Plan

Hybrid picking can be hard on the fingertips at first if you haven't developed callouses. Therefore, I recommend doing this routine every second day or in short intervals, alternating between other routines for this week's practice.

Whether you pluck with the skin of the fingertips only or include a little fingernail for extra chirp, focus firstly on good tone and accurate timing, applying speed incrementally from day to day or over several repeats of the routine.

Included in the video content is an eight-minute bonus lesson on building your hybrid picking. Here's your tempo training routine for the week. As the first few exercises get too easy, drop them and focus on the latter examples.

Drill	Tempo 1 Reps	Tempo 2 Reps	Tempo 3 Reps
Example 8a	2 x (16 bars)	2 x (16 bars)	2 x (16 bars)
Example 8b	2 x (16 bars)	2 x (16 bars)	2 x (16 bars)
Example 8c	3 x (12 bars)	3 x (12 bars)	3 x (12 bars)
Example 8d	3 x (12 bars)	3 x (12 bars)	3 x (12 bars)
Example 8e	3 x (12 bars)	3 x (12 bars)	3 x (12 bars)
Example 8f	3 x (12 bars)	3 x (12 bars)	3 x (12 bars)
Example 8g	4 x (12 bars)	4 x (12 bars)	4 x (12 bars)
Example 8h	3 x (12 bars)	3 x (12 bars)	3 x (12 bars)
Example 8i	3 x (12 bars)	3 x (12 bars)	3 x (12 bars)

Next week, we'll add one more technique (two-handed tapping) before combining techniques and wrapping up with the final etude.

Week Nine: Tapping

This week's tapping workout looks at various applications using single and multiple tapping fingers.

To loosen up, here's a classical-sounding etude executed with taps from both hands in a repeated pattern.

Indicated by circled T symbols, the fretting hand handles power chords with the first and third fingers. These notes are held down while the tapping hand adds two more chord tones with the first and second fingers, outlining the chord progression indicated.

For stability, the thumb of my tapping hand (picking hand) rests on the side of the neck and slides up and down according to where the tapped notes are located.

Example 9a:

Using fingers one, two and three of both hands, the next drill spells out a B diminished 7th arpeggio – a good warmup for both hands, and a strength builder if you've never tapped with the third finger before.

Example 9b:

While many people think of "licks" when it comes to tapping, I like to address it as a technique that has its own freedom and flow, improvising with it in the same way I might with purely fretting-hand legato.

Here's a Reb Beach-style motif moving up the fretboard positionally in the key of C Major. One tapping finger (the first, in my case) replaces the weaker fretting hand fourth finger. Beach uses the second tapping finger instead.

Example 9c:

Incorporating slides this time, here's a quintuplet sequence that moves down the top three strings.

Rhythmically, the idea is to land each tapping note dead-on the beat, and it's up to you how strictly you time the other notes or whether you want more of a rubato, push-pull sort of phrasing.

Example 9d:

```
T        T        T        T        T        T        T
  16-14-12-10-12-14-12-10-9-10-12-10-9-7-9-10-9-7-5-7 | 9-7-5-4-5-7-5-4-2-4-5-4-2
T        T        T        T        T        T        T
```

Initiated with a single downstroke on each string, the next tapping lick uses three fretting hand notes plus a tapped extension.

Since you'll be holding the pick throughout, you can tap with your second finger, or tap with the first and switch your pick grip to the thumb and second finger.

Fretting-wise, the sequence is based on a two-string idea that moves up and down in octaves.

On the descent in bars three and four, a hammer-on from nowhere with the fretting hand initiates the string, followed immediately by a tapped note and a row of pull-offs.

Example 9e:

```
                                                    10-12-14-17-14-12-
                     8-10-12-15-12-10-8-10-12-
-8-10-12-15-12-10-8-10-12-
```

```
-10-12-14-                                          13-15-17-
          -10-12-14-17-14-12-10-12-14-
                               13-15-17-20-17-15-13-15-17-
```

For arpeggio vocabulary, here's a form containing three chord tones per string.

Example 9f contains major 7th arpeggios beginning on the sixth string and fifth string, while Example 9g is a transition exercise through four 7th chord types.

Example 9f:

Example 9g:

From my *Rock Guitar Tapping Technique* book, the next drill uses three tapping fingers and two fretting hand fingers.

Changing the notes in each bar to spell out the chords indicated, all notes are hammered on without picking. To keep the transcription clean, I've omitted tapping indicators for the fretting hand, so that you can see clearly where the right-hand taps occur.

The unusual melodic figure and left/right-hand interplay make this drill quite a challenge, so take it slow to internalise the sequence.

Example 9h:

The final drill in the routine uses power-chord shapes fretted with both hands to spell out major 7th and minor 7th arpeggios.

By moving the tapping hand a fret lower in bars three and four, the 3rd and 7th degrees of the arpeggio are lowered from major to minor intervals.

Example 9i:

Week Nine Practice Plan

This week, the plan uses the first two drills as warmups, the next five licks for tempo training, and the last two for multi-finger coordination.

The audio provides sonic references for the kinds of tones I use for each example, with a clean variety of tones for examples 9a, 9b and 9i, and enough overdrive to get sustain and compression for the remaining examples.

Whatever your tonal preference, ensure you get nice volume and consistency from your left- and right-hand taps.

For the lead-lick-oriented tapping material, I encourage you to spend some time just tapping away in a stream-of-consciousness way, letting the ideas flow, and aiming to find your voice within the tapping approach.

Here's the practice plan:

Drill	Tempo 1 Reps	Tempo 2 Reps	Tempo 3 Reps
Example 9a	Warmup	-	-
Example 9b	Warmup	-	-
Example 9c	3 x (12 bars)	3 x (12 bars)	3 x (12 bars)
Example 9d	3 x (12 bars)	3 x (12 bars)	3 x (12 bars)
Example 9e	3 x (12 bars)	3 x (12 bars)	3 x (12 bars)
Example 9f	3 x (12 bars)	3 x (12 bars)	3 x (12 bars)
Example 9g	2 x (16 bars)	2 x (16 bars)	2 x (16 bars)
Example 9h	Free time	-	-
Example 9i	Free time	-	-

With any leftover time, construct a revision routine comprised of the modified practice drills in Week Seven (examples 7a to 7g).

In next week's routine, we'll run through a way of playing arpeggios that differs from the sweep-picking routine in Week Six.

Week Ten: String Skipping Arpeggios

Rather than introducing a new technique for this chapter, I want to give you another great mechanical approach for playing arpeggios: string skipping.

For the uninitiated, the string-skipping arpeggio options in this chapter allow some sequencing and dynamic options that would be difficult to get with sweep picking.

Let me walk you through it. Examples in this routine are mostly from the key of E Major.

Here's a comparison between a four-string E Major triad sweep (bars one and two) and the string-skipping counterpart (bars three and four).

By simply changing the location of the B note from the 12th fret of the second string to the 16th fret of the third string, we get a shape that feels almost pentatonic in its layout.

Example 10a:

Going beyond simple ascending and descending triads, string-skipping allows for some cool sequencing that would be quite a nightmare to sweep pick. Moreover, we can increase the dynamic range of the sequence by including hammer-ons and pull-offs.

Example 10b:

Next, alter the previous shape to get minor and diminished triads.

Example 10c:

To make things more challenging and musical, here's a progression and sequence from the key of E Major using the three triad shapes covered so far.

Beyond the shapes that run from the fourth string to the first string, I've also ventured into the octave down, between the fifth and second strings.

The shapes in the lower octave are the same but on the lower set of strings.

Example 10d:

Many people use string skipping with the triad shapes in the last couple of examples, but in my practice, I decided to delve a little deeper and seek out some other chord types.

Here's a transition exercise I came up with that includes augmented, major, minor and diminished triads, as well as suspended 4th and suspended 2nd arpeggios.

Example 10e:

Seventh arpeggios also work well with string skipping, although the geometry is a bigger challenge.

Here's another transition exercise from Emaj7 to Edim7 arpeggios, changing one note at a time to move through the other chord types.

Example 10f:

In writing this workout, I wanted to diverge from the format of having the root note on the fourth string, two notes on the third string, and so forth.

As a final transition exercise, I developed this form that works from the sixth string.

This time, each arpeggio is played from a C root note. You can articulate this with any choice of pick strokes and slurs. I'm opting for alternate picking on the audio for some picking practice.

By the way, in case you're wondering why I opted for "B double flat" notes in bar nine, it's because the diminished chord construction is 1, b3, b5, bb7. The last note sounds like an A, but Bbb is the correct usage here.

Example 10g:

For the final part of this routine, we'll use string-skipping triad shapes as enclosures for melodic ideas that include scale notes between chord tones.

For instance, the E Major triad in bar one houses the non-chord tones of the A note on the 14th fret of the third string and F# on the 14th fret of the first string. Each triad has passing tones in similar locations relative to the chord tones.

Executed with mostly alternate picking, this small etude makes a great workout for the picking hand, too.

Example 10h:

Week Ten Practice Plan

Use the first day of the practice week to examine the shapes in this chapter, then use the first example to warm up, and the remainder of the routine for tempo training.

Drill	Tempo 1 Reps	Tempo 2 Reps	Tempo 3 Reps
Example 10a	Warmup	-	-
Example 10b	3 x (12 bars)	3 x (12 bars)	3 x (12 bars)
Example 10c	3 x (12 bars)	3 x (12 bars)	3 x (12 bars)
Example 10d	3 x (24 bars)	3 x (24 bars)	3 x (24 bars)
Example 10e	3 x (24 bars)	3 x (24 bars)	3 x (24 bars)
Example 10f	3 x (18 bars)	3 x (18 bars)	3 x (18 bars)
Example 10g	2 x (20 bars)	2 x (20 bars)	2 x (20 bars)
Example 10h	3 x (24 bars)	3 x (24 bars)	3 x (24 bars)

Once you've familiarised yourself with the drills in this routine, you might also like to experiment with your own picking choices, using more legato or your own choice of chord progressions.

The concept can and should be applied in whatever way you feel is your own.

Next, technique combos to begin the all-important task of stacking techniques into single licks.

Week Eleven: Technique Combos

For this routine, I've written a series of fun shred-style combination licks, bringing together many of the previous concepts into musical phrases to be used in your solos. All licks are in the key of A Major.

By this point, you'll already have the skills to perform these licks, but the combinations and finer details might take some work.

Let's begin with a series of legato and picking combos in examples 11a to 11d.

This first combo lick is straight out of the Edward Van Halen playbook. Eddie was not a strict alternate picker like, say, Al Di Meola, but he had a cool approach that was used in the Van Halen classic, *Spanish Fly*.

A dynamic contrast is created by following hammer-ons with muted picking in a six-note motif.

The first six notes of Example 11a can be looped to get the hang of the lick before you try it in each repeating octave.

Example 11a:

Here's a descending counterpart to the previous drill. You can also reverse the execution of either lick so that the muted picking comes first, followed by a pick stroke and two slurs.

Example 11b:

In the Paul Gilbert style, another picking/legato combo is played in two octaves. Once you know the sequence, try it with other scales and modes.

I play this with the most direct pick strokes, but if you want an even more overt Gilbert attack, reverse the pick strokes to outside picking, then accent each of the picked notes to create a bigger variance in dynamics.

Example 11c:

Here's an economy-picking run this time, played in unusual groupings to create a rushed time feel. You can listen to the audio for my take on this run, but the most important aspects of the lick are the efficient economy picking and the contrast between the legato and muted picking portions on the way down.

Example 11d:

We combined sweep picking with both alternate and economy-picked scale lines in the early weeks of this bootcamp but haven't done so with legato until now.

Below, a position-shifting A Major triad leads to a descending legato sequence, ending with another ascending triad sweep. You can begin each string in the legato sequence with a hammer-on from nowhere or a pick stroke.

Example 11e:

A sweep picking and tapping combination, Example 11f uses mirrored shapes between hands.

From the 3rd beat of bar one, you'll tap the notes of an E Major triad in the 16th position, pulling off to the same triad shape in the 9th position (A Major) with the fretting hand.

Hammer-ons from nowhere initiate each string on the way down before adding a tapping finger hammer-on and pull-off.

In bars three and four, the same lick is moved up one chord in the key, using a B Minor triad with the fretting hand and F# Minor chord tones for the tapped notes.

If you're sweep picking the regular way with the pick held between your thumb and first finger, tap with the second finger.

Example 11f:

For the final lick in the routine, we'll combine string skipped and sweep-picked A Major triads with a picking and legato scale sequence.

Besides being a lot of fun, this lick will have you changing techniques, dynamics, and subdivisions throughout.

Example 11g:

By this point, you're well familiar with the concept of the tempo-training practice plan, so there's little point in having another one for this material.

What I'd like you to do this week is to take your four favourite licks from this chapter, practice them up and get as comfortable as you can, then come back for the rest.

The main process to take note of in this chapter is how I've gone about combining approaches from earlier in the book. Now, see how you can do the same with licks of your own.

To take the idea of combinations a step further, your mission for the final two weeks of the bootcamp is to study the solo etude in the last chapter.

Weeks Twelve and Thirteen: Final Etude

To combine and apply the techniques from this bootcamp to actual music, I present you with a piece I call *Vinnie MacAlpsteen*.

Fusing the skills of players like Vinnie Moore, Tony Macalpine, and Yngwie Malmsteen, this solo in the key of E Minor will be a shredder's delight as it contains sweep-picked arpeggios, picking sequences, pedal-tone licks, tapping, and octave-based patterns.

Rather than taking up pages breaking down the licks in this solo, I've prepared a video lesson that is included with the bonus streaming content for this book.

The video breaks the solo into sections, with musical descriptions and slowed-down performances.

The backing track is included in the audio download.

When practicing this piece, treat each section like the licks in the other chapters. Learn the song in phrases, tempo-train those phrases in stages, then combine the pieces again to perform the solo at a slow pace, then gradually faster.

There are thirty bars in the piece, so even if you focused on two bars per day, that's fifteen days until you've covered everything. With the techniques you've practiced for the previous eleven weeks, you're in a far better position to master this material now than if I'd just given you the solo a few months ago.

Test your ability by aiming for full speed, then go back to work on any parts that aren't up to the standard of the others.

Best of luck learning the piece!

"Vinnie MacAlpsteen"

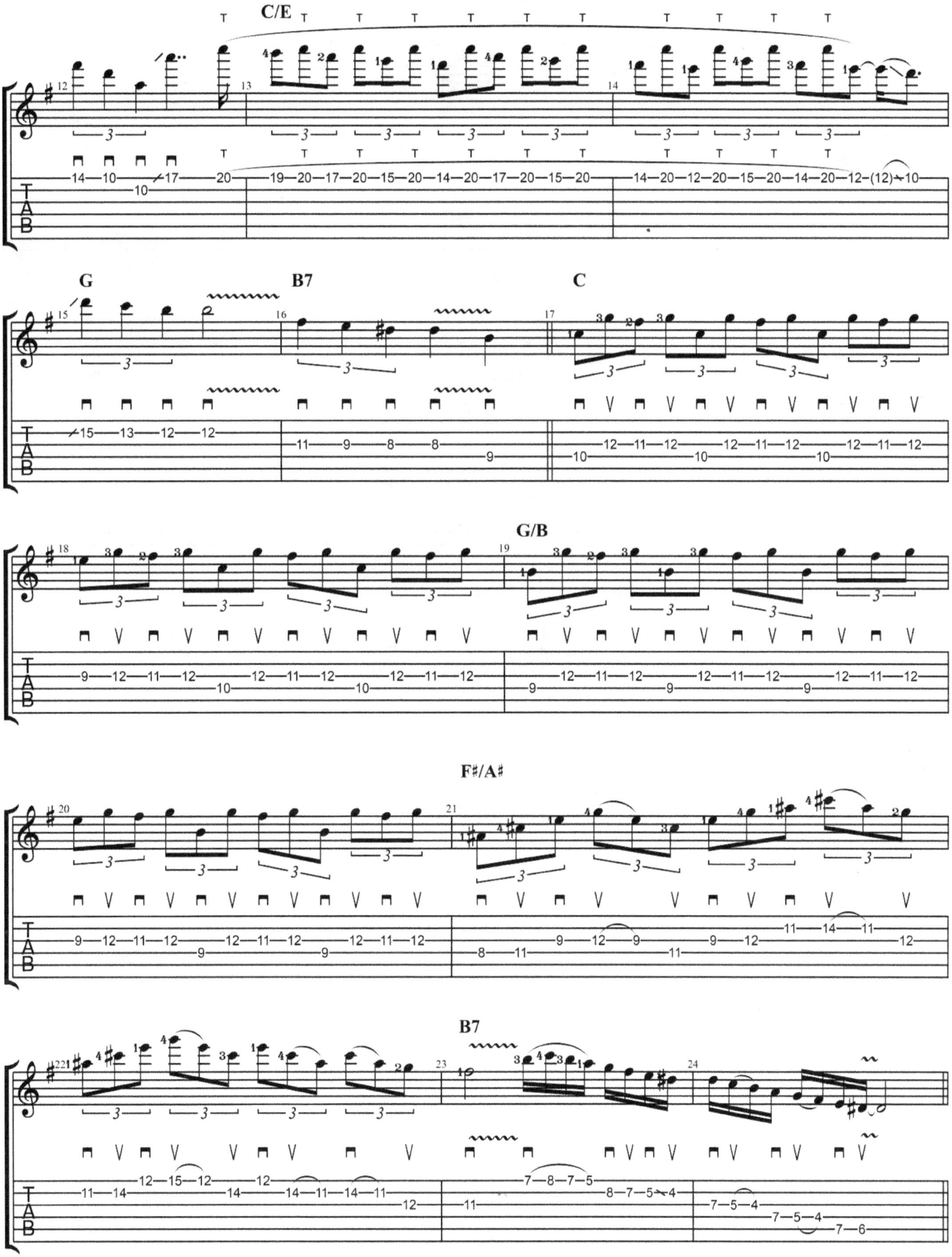
C/E
G
B7
C
G/B
F♯/A♯
B7

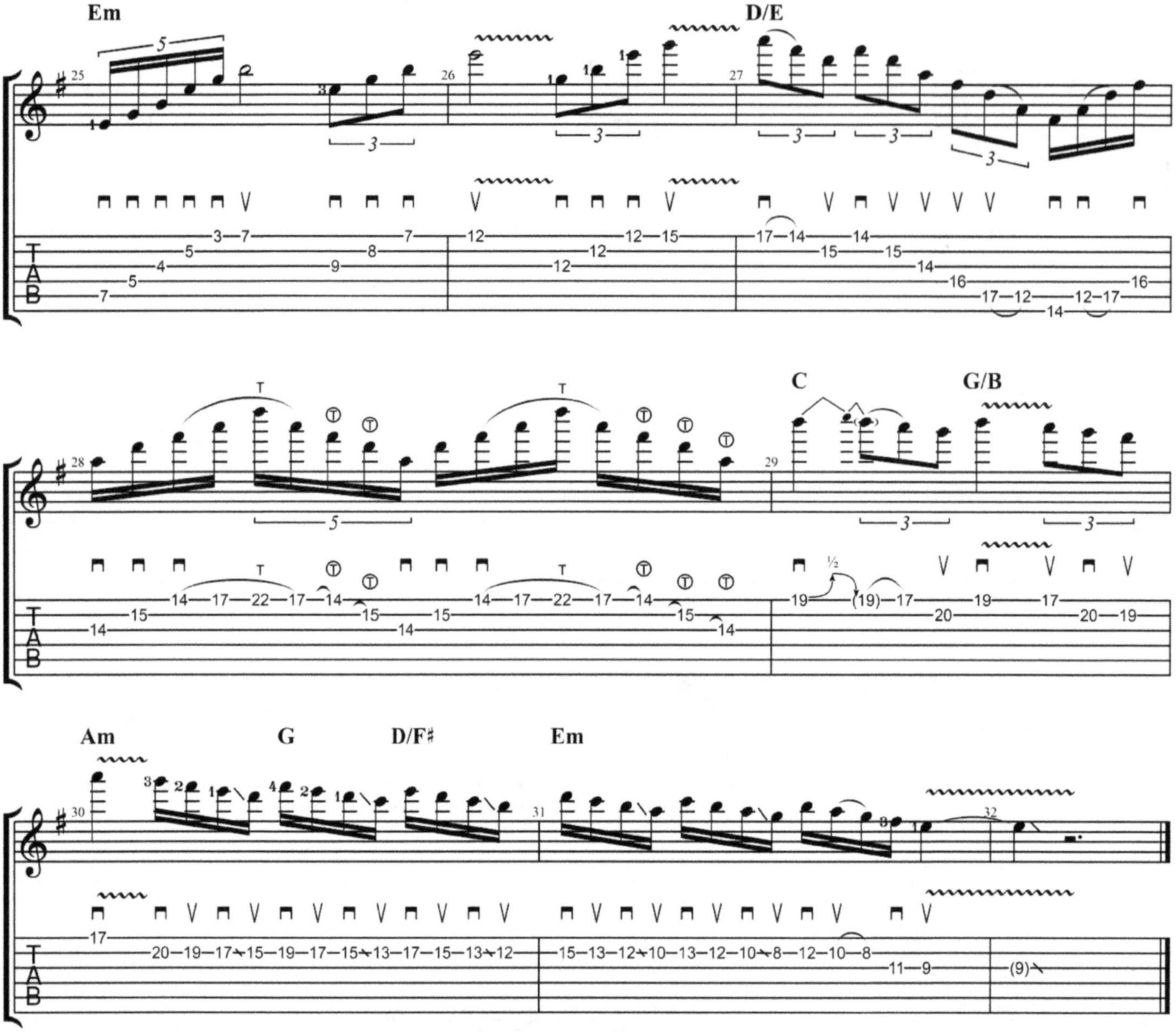
Em
D/E
C
G/B
Am
G
D/F♯
Em

Conclusion

This brings us to the end of not only this book but also my trilogy of technique practice books!

I hope you've gained a lot of insight into the techniques contained in these pages and, more importantly, learned how to address advanced concepts through a daily practice format that is both achievable and flexible.

While the format of the book is based on thirteen weeks, some players may need to run the program a few times or revisit chapters on techniques that they have less experience with – and that's okay! There are some techniques I got lucky with over a few months and others that took years.

When judging your results, the question to ask yourself is, "Did I get better in the last few months?"

If you stuck to the plans and worked diligently, I'm confident you will answer in the affirmative.

The next step in any technique is to build more vocabulary to prevent being limited in where you can use it. For example, now that you can sweep pick, it would be useful to know the eighty arpeggio shapes in my *Sweep Picking Speed Strategies* book.

If your legato is going great guns now, *Legato Guitar Technique Mastery* will help you level up with a plethora of rock and fusion legato licks and patterns.

The thing about success is that it's often contagious. When you get one technique to a high level, you have a process for getting better at the next one.

For anything that needs to go "back to formula," you have the resources to revise and rebuild a better technique via this series and my other books.

On the last page of the book, you'll see a list of my current catalogue with Fundamental Changes. To go deeper into any subject, grab the book that interests you and apply the same practice principles you adhered to in this bootcamp.

If you want to plan and track your practice routines, I recommend using a diary, like my *365-day Music Practice Planner*, available on Amazon.

Thanks for giving me these thirteen weeks to guide and inform your daily guitar work.

Chris Brooks

About the Author

Chris Brooks has set new standards for the calibre of guitar technique books. With a flair for what makes things tick, his depth of understanding of guitar mechanics has helped tens of thousands of readers across the world.

Playing guitar since September 1987, Chris took early inspiration from Brett Garsed, Kee Marcello, Vinnie Moore, and Yngwie Malmsteen, practicing feverishly through his teens.

Educated at the Australian Institute of Music under the tutelage of Dieter Kleeman, Ike Isaacs, and Carl Orr, Chris developed a passion for guitar education that resulted in managing a music school with close to a thousand private students per week in Sydney's western suburbs.

Focusing on online education and product development in the last decade, Chris has now written more than a dozen bestselling guitar books, created scores of video products, and released two acclaimed instrumental rock albums.

You can learn more at **www.chrisbrooks.com**

Other titles by Chris Brooks

Neoclassical Speed Strategies for Guitar

Sweep Picking Speed Strategies for Guitar

Advanced Arpeggio Soloing for Guitar

7-string Sweep Picking Speed Strategies for Guitar

Legato Guitar Technique Mastery

100 Arpeggio Licks for Shred Guitar

The Complete Guitar Technique Speed Strategies Collection

Alternate Picking Guitar Technique

Economy Picking Guitar Technique

Rock Guitar Tapping Technique

Chris Brooks' 3-in-1 Picking & Tapping Guitar Technique Collection

137 Guitar Speed & Coordination Exercises

Pentatonic Speed Strategies for Guitar

1980s Rock Rhythm Guitar Mastery

Guitar Practice Warmup Routines

Thirteen Week Guitar Technique Bootcamp – Intermediate Level